i

c

o

p

e

DUMBHEART/ STUPIDFACE

Cooper Wilhelm

1. *Everyone Had Feelings and Everyone's Feelings Were Wrong.*

| Postscript

I transcribe poems of mine I can mostly read
from a notebook
with the painstaking frustration of a Dickinson scholar
who is also Emily Dickinson with amnesia
from having lost the world,
and I begin to think I won't like being dead.

Not for the boring reasons
about worms and people
who can't love you enough because how could they

know what it's like to say nothing in a kitchen one winter morn-
ing,
light thrown across the table like a scarf,
but because in the afterlife I'd like to hang out

with Frank O'Hara and James Schuyler and I suspect
I won't be invited to those parties.

It's fine. There are options.
There aren't.

But:
I could be the voice you hear in your head
but don't hear
when almost buying movie theater nachos, or hitting whiskey

#8,
or listening to love songs you don't want to believe.

Most likely, I'll end up eating Sunday lunch with Longfellow,
avuncular, burn-bearded man from my hometown,
who may be a bad influence insomuch as he loves Dante
for possibly the wrong reasons, and chose
to be an old man even in paradise.

And when I die they will say
Connor, you're dead
and I will not correct them
because I will be dead.

Non-existence terrifies me
almost as much as the idea of living

in a world without words,
but I'm glad you didn't pick up
so I could tell you all this.

And since it's already later
just think:
Wherever you are
I could be on my way.

|Everyone I've spoken to doesn't want you to succeed.

Aphorism 1:
When starting down the path of love, dig two graves.

Aphorism 1:
They're both for you.

I never in my life believed a thing that wasn't trying to kill me.
Most restaurants have a back door through the kitchen.
Some fire escapes only take you to the roof.
The ladder back up to the platform
is usually located near the front end of the train.
Love always ends
in an open grave or in a shut blossom
and you don't need claws
to tease your body out.

| Le Grand Dérangement

I wandered through the kitchen
moonwoke, the wood cold as wet grass.
I've never been to your muggy NOLA,
but here's a cup
from some Mardi Gras
you went to before going without me
would make sense
as a thing to get sore at.
Proverbs says stolen waters are sweet,
and bread eaten in secret
is pleasant.
Cool water can be worth the journey
it makes you forget
I guess.
Four months later,
and I've found the sink.

| Poem of a Monologue Spoken by One Partner to Another to Comfort Both After Both Have Made a Good-Faith Effort to Make Things Work, to be Open and Vulnerable While Still Balancing Self-Care with Support and Celebration of the Other — and After Both Have, Together and Separately, Come to the Tumorous Conclusion that What Each Needs is Not the Other and that to be Apart From the Other, Though Love and Complete Understanding of the Other (as Far as that is Ever Possible) Will Likely Persist in Each for Years — and After the Despair at Knowing that, Even if Either Partner Should One Day Find a Love that Similarly Takes them Out of Themselves While Reassuring them that they Do Actually Belong in the World, it will be Tainted by this Failure to be in Perfect Love, and at Knowing that Each Has Done this to Themselves and the Other, has Led to Brief Flashes of Cruelty, the Claws of the Starving, the Most Dangerous Animals being the Wounded Ones — and After Realizing that the Time has Come to Release Themselves from the Duty to Protect even the Possibility of Hope as Far as the World of this Relationship and all its Possible Variations, its whole Multiverse of What Could Be, is Concerned — and having Argued this Point with themselves without Success Until at Last Arguing it with Sufficient Success to Momentarily Silence but Not Erase All Doubts.

| Burn the rise.

I thought there would be burning, a black star
branded on the floor around my empty shoes
as if all the world were at last a map.

Who knows how long
ago she filled the machine
with barely sound enough to say
press 1 for an emergency. It doesn't count. It will wait
out longer than anything I've had, anything
that's mine.

| Hummock Bark

Un
-lucky promises. Here's where good things go get desperate.

Please, somebody, listen to me:
I met Broomhilda milking spiders in the holy den,
making naked worship on low-hung branches,
peeling newts and bones.
Stones of quality, unlike the others in wood,
plagioclase, aplite, feldspar, litchfieldite,
obsidian, breccia, marl,
adakite, granophyre
were our hungry bed.

All the while the quilt was lurking
to clot us in remorseless love,
bilkless savor, hot piddle, plucking moles
and blackheads in a bathroom mirror
that looks out on an open door.
On our buried bodies in the loving cot,
built we stick by stick the wind-pulled cabin
of trust, wove our home wherever we was.

What's love? A stick of lead in your coat pocket? A shallow
boat?
The empty glove, lost, stuck,

too wet to keep warm in a puddle that will cut
from ear to ear its hole with ice.

Broomhilda, just tonight, live me be, and lift
the gnarled wishbone, no-spite curse
of being in these woods beside you but always out of sight.

| Mange Ways

18.9 herz is a frequency that can induce hallucinations
by rippling the eyeball's crystal goo, by which I mean scientifi-
cally
its flavored gel not unlike KY spun
and tinctured with an element of rust.
18.9 herz is hidden in a tiger's roar and hearing it reminds us
death swoops down to meet us like a pigeon
leaving the top shelf of a bookcase in a haunted mansion
owned by a deceased uncle we never met but who left it to us
on the condition we risk our lives inside it for just one night
at which point we earn the right to risk our lives inside it until
we die
which is sort of like forever.
That's the nature of every compact.
That's nature in every compact.
But this is a digression. I am teaching you
with discipline that Prokofiev would eat only addled eggs,
which is to say eggs from which the chickens could not get
loose
and thus died still hidden like facehuggers
rotting in the cage of an unlucky space truck driver.
I have invented this detail about Prokofiev to make him or her
statistically
more accessible to adults of all ages here's a graph.
no need to thank me I can't help

myself here's another graph wait
here there are more still in my car
don't go.

Please there is so much to tell you.
Fear is the petri dish where angels grow.

| Himmel Oder

On the morning when she climbs up
from the bed, a metronome of tan lines,
and does not come back.
On the morning when you consider simple questions
you did not ask, the whys and hows
of being someone other than yourself.

There will always be a journey to undertake
an influence to thwart, a heart to win back.
When Sybaris fell to pipe players,
and was spread over by a silken flame,
the light swallowing patina
from the old brass roofs turned blue
like it was just another festival,
no one left indoors,
the colts still wallowing in their dance.

| Travel Advisory: Minos

I've prepared a brief bar napkin
with some things you should say to me:

> ¤ *Your fear is an animal you hide in a labyrinth.*

> ¤ *You feed your fear*
> *parts of complex human beings.*

I am coughing up a red feather
looking anywhere but the empty cage.

> ¤ *You make everything you touch another sociopath.*

The parrot in my chest repeats the full transcript
of things you've actually said
for me to practice on.   Karaoke for one
        part to be rewritten.

The parrot helps me believe   that when the
person I still am
       crashes through the levy and throws
    us back into our lives
          I will deserve it
          and you will

deserve it

because the warning signs were there.

Loneliness is coming to save us from this temporary self.

The dirt and stone is rushing

up to save me

from looking for the drop.

| We think we can see inside a diamond without tearing it apart.

And when the wall looks green
because of light reflected off grass
outside the window, or looks red
because you parked your honda
on the street, it is green
and it is red.

I don't know which parts of you
I'm already adding to my me,
bright fishing line woven into a nest.

Tell my body to me again with your fingers.

| Ἀγάπη **No More**

Apparently I love you, but that's not a plan.
I walk 84 blocks and can talk to the woman
behind the counter at the place near your apartment with precision
about the kind of coffee I want, can hold the whole cup,
can remember my lips and how to find them.
When you lose all of your senses all the others get better,

but getting there is hard and I have rent to consider,
sainthood essentially serving as an internship in which,
because you work in love,
no one ever pays.

The whole of this wicked world felt like a house party
that wouldn't let me in, windows shaming
the snow outside with summer light.

But all that is over now because I love you,
and probably will for the next three days.
And after that death I will rise,
and after that I will love you, and so on,
until my throat fills up with autumn leaves,
and even then I will text you
things for you to bless better than I ever could.

| Golden Bricks of Café Bustelo

My first time alone in your apartment
and I'm tripping over everything.
11 minutes to decipher how the shower works,
doing all the dishes so I don't leave my glass
for you to find someday in the sink.

I have no right to hear this voice.
It is plainly reasonable to believe each time I see you
is the time you will say you want to be exclusive
with everyone who isn't me.

But I'll make a few more cups of coffee,
the rest of the bag, just so I can leave
a note telling you I'll grab a little more
next time I come over.

|4 AM

Das naß, warm Herz drängt sich die Lippen ein.
(The wet, warm heart pushes in past the lips.)

When you speak, the handlebars fall off my chest.
I become feathers scattered from your voice,
a thousand separate things that could never fly

but together might make a pillow.

Anyone can make avocado toast
even a man who has no hands
because he has donated his hands
to a charity for people without hands
for which he would now be eligible
because he has no hands.

This is me trying to tell you about the hot stone
in my mouth. Sloppy breakfast.
No better than anyone else could do
but I'm doing it now
even if you're not awake.

| Summations end.

I.

Since Thursday I've come around to the idea that I could be in
love
and still keep my life. I've been wondering if it can't be like
plying a marker
to a map, making all the daily roads brighter and thick as blood
vessels heavy with traffic trucking hand-in-hand with precious
air.
This is not because of you.

II.

The chief of police says we are treating
all threats as credible. But based on a recent poll
of things I've seen today, mostly in the woods,
I'm easy and ready,
just say hi.

It is the fifth of July
and I am allowed to be sad again.
At least until Christmas.
But even misery is unfair,
the wound we want so badly to be seen,
and I don't think about the way effort
makes a hummingbird's wings invisible, hiding the methods

and engines of, despite gravity and everything,
staying exactly where it was and when.
It is a man trying to carve a boat out of buckets
of storm water.
But I have forgotten all that and never refer to the maps
the act of highlighting makes you read, even though you know
the places from the limited perspective of your daily life.

III.

Once a woman in a car told me that she met Glenn Danzig
once
and also that when she gave birth she didn't know
she was giving birth to fear.
Sometimes I wish God had the grace of just one duckling
ripping larvae from the downy mud
that was hidden until the spotless sun cooked off its lake
like pulling back a sheet. Instead the good lord lets us think
there are things
that we can keep, even in the immortal terror of being seen,
every muscle,
every blade of you unable to stop itself
from coming to be known.

I've been in love twice, not at the same time,
and the woman in the car said I could quote her.
My life has started to feel like one long fourth act
in which nothing is decided and all good outcomes are unlikely.

The detectives have already failed,
and there is no climax, but I am old enough that
I can eat ice cream for every meal until I die. Here we go.

IV.

Falling in love should be like skidding backwards
out of an airplane: accidental, no takebacks,
and with an unspoken guarantee manifest to all involved
that I will fly through the ending scattered
and destroyed and free of myself.

V.

Cars sound so fast when they struggle.
They announce their own A for effort
no matter where they are directed to go.
There's so much you can owe someone
which is to say I have too much shame in me
to indulge in the self-confidence of panic.
Turn my own music down.
Everything slides back the lake
and nothing from the dark is sacred or protected.
Neither rocks, nor worms, nor eggs wrinkled like faces in the
evil light.

Here we go.

2. *Index Crimes*

| Consider dying in an important fire.

Ransom Note 1

In the beginning I saw your body
as a rowboat, tears
up to the ankles, troubles cooled over
into suet,
into chelev for each new day. Such soft
and marbled things you ferried with you,
ready to melt the moment
they were needed.
Name the lake you paddle most
and it will still replace you.
Name the snakes you made and they will follow you
or not. Name stars in what arrangements
remind you of yourself. What could they ever
do to stop you?

Ransom Note 2

Consider dying in a fire
set by history and how
this would enunciate you better
than a million thought-out deeds.
An exact disclosure of my other demands will be withheld
until further notice. You should cooperate.
I am troubled with the attention
other men receive
from the detectives. I watch them
sit in their cars, drink coffee,
unwrap their private heartaches like egg salad,
grease on their wax paper, the glint of other wives.
Whose hostage should we be?

I am the one who'd drink the color from your eyes.
This man does no one any good. He asks for silence
without being interesting.
He should walk into a forest
and wait until he becomes flowers.

<u>Ransom Note 4</u>

We have met. Neither of us will be remembered.
But we have met.

Ransom Note 4

In costume for the Ghost Dance, in season for the scythe,

I am the wandering planet, Nibiru. I will be discovered too late.

Step out of the flames to meet me.

Do the police follow me on twitter?

I've stopped using computers. There is no difference on the
internet

between a network and a shopping list.

Algorithms will approve new dates and the meting out of days,

someone will endorse the skillsets yet unseen

and knight me with a coffee spoon.

The police may never ask who is he with now

if not with us.

After all I've done to fill their lives with content,

with the honey of congealed days,

thickened light ready for the archives!

This is how rejection works.

I want you to believe me.

Please do not know my name.

There are real things you can do today

and never hear from me again.

Ransom Note 4

I am Nibiru. I will touch the cradle of life
and by coming too close
make a furnace
where even stones escape us
as white clouds.
We will never meet.
Do not know my name.

| Koan

A girl decides to walk around her neighborhood
and after several turns down streets she'd never been on
because they were never on the way
she turns to see the raised buttocks of a man she hates.
His shoulders wriggle behind the horizon of his hips,
his bathrobe getting smutty,
as he nurtures the roots of a beach rose nestled by his porch.
Her mind is no longer a play interrupting from the background.
Only purpose as she strides to her neighbor's place upon the
grass,
raises up her foot in full expression of the leg,
and brings her heel down on his neck.
You could say that she'll appraise
her neighbor now is likely dead, but it's more
the way a person looking at the sky
knows without consideration it will rain.
She plucks a rose berry in this moment and she bites
careful not to eat the little hairs inside.

| Suet Moss

Now is a time to talk to Adam's other wives.
The apocalypse may be the last frontier
for lucrative investment.
Brutal economics taught me how to make out,
how to fear my body (the Bible helped)
how to fear my body (my body helped)
how to build a face to meet the faces that will decide again and
again
every microsecond if my debts will qualify
to sponge the muscles from my bones.
With these loans release yourself from acne;
the GDP eternal summons You!

Forgive me. Now is an era of humiliation.
Decay is always transactional, we live
in a glass globe we cannot break.
Definition of Decay: *Everything is preserved*
in commerce through the system.
P R E D A T O R
S A V O I R   M E A T
It should release me.

The bankers extolled their virtues,
the administrators of the education
said even bakers must post resumes forever.
They have gotten what they wanted. All of this

is meant. All
of this is good. I watch my friends
get flattened into baseball cards
and gloss and stats and traded.
People I have braved are now,
have always been, a given thing
passed across the networks like minerals dissolved,
fungi piping them into the roots of trees
for sugar from their leaves. Each species
another specie of decay.

The powerful only see the rarified parts of you
they eat, the soot upon the altar plate.
The system lies dreaming, its heart pumping blood
in modelable patterns on displays.
All of this was made. All of this
is good. All of this is meant.
Another species of decay
like breath.

Fear teaches us to keep our bodies clean and fragrant.
Fear is the kindness of a society
that laughs at you for having flesh,
for not being photoshopped onto the unknown beaches.
Sing yourself into a clean thing,
dry smoke forsaking viscera.

Adam couldn't handle seeing
the second one being built from the same eyes
and entrails he couldn't see inside himself.
So she just dies. The good lord's mercy.
But she was, remember, a retry.
Stepping shoeless through the canon
the details shift from side to side,
but some things stay where they were planted.
God's a we, a man's an I, and what's one
human life?
This is the important question—
God's a boxed-up cat forever (until we die)
and Adam named the animals,
that's enough for them—
Lilith has always been the one
to ask.

Lilith takes those who sleep alone.
May she carry us into her house
from which none can find again the paths of life.
Talmudic scholars maintain she has sex with monsters
because she refused to be a helpmate serving a stranger
made from the same dirt. Good. She could teach us
to gather hawks under our shadows,
to cull from ourselves every fiber that would plead
dull men into power,
into the right to give us back our bodies
when it suits them.

Our eggs are all our own to harvest
and to ply.

These paths of life are not the only paths.
"Her house sinks down to death,
And her course leads to the shades.
All who go to her cannot return." Names
and credit scores will be tools for cannibals
as long as they hold sway.
P R E D A T O R S A V O I R M E A T
The time has come to eat their teeth
and make the bastards watch.

|Marry me, Saint Batman.

This one time, I was some kind of horse
or something (this is a True Story),
and I wept as the gendarmes chained
my hooves with whips.

Marry me, Saint Batman,
launch our crumpled arteries from the canopy
of the old bower, like petals shed in wanting.
I can be a stalwart companion and will lift
my own weight in box springs to please you.
But you will fly away and sing how you can only
be smitten with Finnish liquors and different birds.
I am better off without the superhero
most taken with Ayn Rand.

Aloft!

A Sea Of Bastards! Ugh!

| People I Could Name

The ghost of David Berkowitz comes to me as I eat breakfast
and complains. His neighbor is too demanding.
"True, yes, I am the killer, but I kill on your command, Craig.
Because Craig is Craig, the streets must run with Craig," etc.
I barely have time to listen to my own problems,
but my new stache and loneliness win over a retired cop
and his still-on-duty cousin at the bar.
I buy us six beers. The two light up
and clue me in that the chalk I saw
running out to grab more eggs (flan
is hard) was not as I had thought,
a depthless grave for the most recent victim.
"You die, they just leave you there.
For pictures," says ex-detective Chuck.
"Chalk's for when you could still be alive,
so they set it down before they pick you up."
It's totemic. You leave your silhouette to lie
enacting death so you can see what new person
medicine will make of you.
Not to dwell on it.

Prehistoric hunters picked up on the idea
that if you drew the animal you wanted it
would link you to some citizen of the species.
Chained to the image, it could only die,
and anyone could be a prophet.

Every night Berkowitz lights a fire so he can call
the cops and no one thanks him. He picks up
extra shifts in his cab. People tip him,
but they don't mean it.

Same outline, different positions.
People used to be better
at believing in monsters. Food was food.
Their neighbors didn't scare them.

What was David's body
count? 8?
With a gun designed to safely kill someone
in an airplane, even in the cockpit.
There were 1,080 terror attacks in the US between 1970 and
1975
and he barely hurt anyone.
But he wrote to the papers.
He got the eyes.
I try to tell the cops,
but by then I've lost
the thread of how the ideas of things relate
to the things themselves.
It's terrible what these kids are doing says Chuck's cousin
I think meaning k2 or kneeling during songs.

The cops drop a bomb on a house in Philadelphia,
run over Branch Davidians in a tank,

but they take David Berkowitz alive,
Jeff Dahmer alive
Eng alive, Lake alive,
Manson, Bundy, Gein, Rahami,
Lucas, Roof, Alive Alive Alive.
And somehow a thousand men and women,
armed with just their lives,
people the papers will never name enough,
were too much to lay hands on and hold
even for judgment before the law.

3. *False Etymologies*

| Prayer to Francis Wilhelm

When Marco Polo at last arrived,
pale from his passage in the mountains,
did Kubla Kahn immediately take him
for an emissary of the dead?
What would the dead trade with the living
that they couldn't pick up on the road?

In a letter to my great grandmother, I have decided,
my great grandfather wrote: *meine*
Herzlose,
endlich vermisse ich dich.

Baby, my heart's been pounding at
your door for hours. I
don't think
you've heard a thing.

I don't know much about my great grandfather,
which means I get to make it,
for the most part, up.
Hessian, like the headless horseman,
but not headless.

I've seen him in a photo grinning in
a three-piece suit in
the shadows in

the back end
of a beach.

Somehow I can't imagine him screaming
back to children as they climb
through the waves and call the name
of a dead explorer trying
to locate themselves.

| On the body lingers.

Maybe a comet will save us.
I assume I shiver in my sleep, like you said,
a shiver for a heartbeat,
despite what I leave
like withered needles on the bedspread,
dead grass on the sheet.

When they light The Empire State Building coal red, it's hard
not to feel like I pay to sleep
in a tight suburb of hell, the eternal sprawl,
the closest waves around the bell.

Dante, in his exile, modeled hell after the city
that wouldn't let him in.
Once I'm dead, I'll have plenty of time to prepare
my mouth for the subtle art of saying nothing.
If you want to fill a hole inside of you,
start charging rent.
That's another thing you said.

At the end of the line,
each of us got 20 seconds alone in the Infinity Room.
You could look this up online: an indoor island,
mirrors fenced the pool,
and both made the Christmas lights
unspooled in the darkness go

on forever for you and you
could breath easy like you knew
even in a world without end
there were limits of the loneliness inside you.

| Leather - Bound

Who   did I steal all this   from to have body, breath,
to bleed.   Carbon, water, phosphorus,
calcium   for bones,
and all the strands   nucleic acid
who command me from the dark wet space.

Sulfur, Lithium.

The earth could not say   no.
The filthiest pools   gasped and bubbled.
Thoughtlessly they formed the rings.

Sodium, magnesium.

And here I curl   up, vertebrate,   enough
to talk.   All.   I grace the world
with only um and sorry.

|They knew too much.

Etymologies are important and apparently their names mean
dust and *the living one*.
The brain glows.

Your blood could kill you and among
the neurons there's an
ugly fuse, quite nestled, ready
for the stroke.

These are the gifts I remember most
from mom and pop, congenital descent,
risk factors calling from the factory floor,
the showcase, the moors,
quiet as a gray hair waiting all night on the pillow.
Or did you just hear yourself listening.

|Titles I Didn't Use for this Book

1. I Was In Love Once! Will No One Praise Me?

2. Fistulated Cow

3. Kwuan Tai Duew Luk Phen

4. A Me Alienum

5. The Thylacine Conspiracy and You

6. I Love You, Please be Nicer to Me

7. The Last of the Horrible Strawberries

8. Conspiracy of Cells

9. Poetry 2: Nemo Found

10. Please Turn into a Flock of Birds

11. Things With Beetles in Them You Put Inside Your Body

12. A Brief Consideration of How Unhappy I Will be When the Time Arrives to Truly be Unhappy.

13. Brace for Break-Up

14. Poetry 2: Dead by Dawn

15. The Incomprehensible Majesty of being Unbearably Sad

16. Too Sad to Write Poems & Half of another poem i guess

17. Things Birds Don't Know that I Don't Know Either

18. Poetry 2: Die Harder

19. This Poem is Also about How Much I Love You, But You are a Metaphor for Cheese.

20. Two Girls, One Cup of Sorrow

21. The Honorable Gretta B. Hawthorne Memorial Rec. Center and Municipal Parking Lot Massacre

22. Only Galactus Can Judge Me

23. The Novel is Dead: A Novel

24. What I Look Like Naked & Additional Photos of Me Naked

25. Please Don't Leave

| Probabilities will collapse.

I.

My grandma loaded
her cupboards with mostly sage and buckshot,
murder and repair, a couple coupons.

The breath that lifted out of her was like incense,
holy with blood,
savory and cedar and rose.

You watch her huff through a smoker's morning cold,
frost everywhere but the leaves still somehow wet,
and see that to sweat is to betray

some humility in the uncouth effort presumably
city folk don't know. Get home.

Bake. Wring your hands around each other
to free them of their dirt. I love you
means so little from a saint
you can let go of not hearing it said that much at home.

II.

Each new day enlightens me
to the entropy of getting old.

The brain and body overstuffed, a trunk your full weight
can't quite close. Just clearing trees.

You provide more space for possibilities,
as in, *given ample time replication will decay*
once in such a way that science must remove a breast
for you to survive;
as in, *if you drive 20 miles each day,*
in a finite and knowable number of days your likelihood of death will rise
from, say,
1 in 2, to 1 in 1, or 2 in 1, though you may still at that moment be alive;

III.

When the old hunters would share a pipe
with a fawn they'd jumped
as a way of saying we are family,
we are family and I remember and I'm sorry.

IV.

as in, *you are more likely to die from your own heart*
or cancer than suicide
suicide than in a car,
in a car than in a space shuttle or plane,
in one of those than from bees or lightening or a dog;
as in, *whenever astronomers or seismologists or studiers of plague*
talk about the next big wave of death
they say from what they know today

could be the day,
we're due.

V.

Grandmother the pipe smoker, throat closed up with bark.
If you listen to the trees make their knock and static,
your brain seeking to please you with patterns,
might make them speak.
Trees or no, my grandmother doesn't speak,
not even in these poems.

| Behold the stout joys of creation.

I know burning makes a better bread
and somewhere between billing and the incinerator
is a kitchen I want to go to.
The first thing I did upon waking in the hospital
was ask about making toast.

Every year until we wipe them from the earth
browntails will hang fogs on trees.
My mother would have them pierced through,
the medicine from the needle just out of reach,

maybe mixing down the iron shaft with fleeting ichor.
She's allergic and their hair dabbed the color from her hands,
turned her skin into a beach pocked over with lost snow.
The whole autumn after, my father watched companies of
them roll
out of the driveway fires he'd loaded
with their silk thrones.

The moon is not enough to stop this.
The sun is not enough.

If you're home, do me a favor:
Light a candle and watch the smoke
until its twisting curdles into moths.

| Slept Through

In the curious generosity of dreams
I am talking to the ghost of Mary Oliver
about what to get the kids
I don't have
for Christmas
while leaning on the sink,
and although I could not repeat a word of what we said to you
because maybe it was just the form of talking
and maybe there are some secrets
my brain will keep,
in talking about it to you now I suddenly remember a wooden
dock,
warm pond water, the cracked,
yellow toenails of my uncle who is dead.
Which is to say my uncle who is gone, which is
to say my uncle
who never
existed, which is
to say
my uncle who is dead.

My uncle who never existed
lives on in phrases like
A long important poop,
in the cloying distinction between like and such as;
in the distinction between such as and such that;

in the distinction between a paycheck and one gasp of air
in a long belt of gasps;
in the distinction between comfort and the cunning
self-deception that keeps you
from meeting the eyes that stare you
down from the inevitable disappointment of your dreams.

Enough distraction.
Three ropes tethered the neck and wrists of my uncle to a tree
stump,
while his brothers pulled at his ankles as at fishing nets
trying to heal his back.

Kids only understand the medicine of pain,
how a new success of suffering
gets it over with;
the splinter dug out with a needle,
from the hand held out
as if to test the rain,
as if to receive a coin
under whose sharp skin sleeps
a lightless room of chocolate.

| Clock and Brambles

After James Wright

I watched down your dirt road
as sparrows casted up their throats
through the autumn cold
and a dead hare hid beneath the oaks.

You were always so much better
than I am at these moments
seeing the skeleton for every bone
before you threw them to winter.

The hare saw your son pressed
by your father's hands
to your chest.

Saw love's fingers sink.
You pulled it apart
so there is nothing to watch.
It's still in the trees.

The rain is leaving footprints deeper
than mine in the dust.
What will you say later about holding my wet shoulders
to feel them push up past the roots each spring?

Your kitchen door was unlocked.
I drifted in with the gray light
that hid from your stove's tiny flame
in the shadows of molded iron.
Fell like an apple from a silent bough.

| Squeeze tight.

If anything is worth doing, it's worth overdoing.
Where was I?
Your mother loved you enough for you to make this cake,
to sell enough catheters to make the house payment,
to finish the job when your 16-year-old hits the cat
with the jetta your mother helped you buy when you left college
for nothing really, nothing, still nothing,
and now this.

4. *Hagiography TK*

| Let us be enchanted.

A copper cross hung just so
as good luck to keep the babies out. Oppenheimer kept
a horseshoe nailed at its arms above his door
like lamb's blood, said,
"They tell me it works
even if you don't believe in it."
He was maybe unaware
that the tradition is a Wiccan way
to bring the Horned Man into the house.
More than unaware, which is to say,
beyond caring, already become
so much more than death.
At any rate,
so reports Žižek.

Reread the old testament enough and you start to focus on the
weird stuff.
There's a recipe, a unicorn, lots of frog, but no kittens,
and no one, it seems, ate cheese
in the truest time of God.

A copper cross hung just so inside her
and a hairless terrier near her bed
swallows everything in a bowl marked "dog."

Such faith. If I believed in God, I'd say
He's one of those things
that works best when you forget they're there,
like potent curves of probabilities
that streak through CERN's chaotic fog, or fatigued policemen
keeping watch, or STIs.

She goes on dates, etc, and it's magic.
She flicks a lighter endlessly,
like a Diogenes uneager to see.
She reads up on shamanism
or "archaic techniques of ecstasy"
(so says Eliade).

Maybe I should believe.
When there is no more light in tenderness,
just closed eyes, just the present throb that fills the room
like a wind to push the world down.
Likening and categories take the messy life from things,
but this feeling could be silence.
This, too, could be God.

|Wächtersteine, Kistvaen,
The Cairn or Excavated Cist

Our human bodies were not ready
for the future. Radium girls with dew drops on their lips,
destined to metastasize; shoe salesmen holding the white bones
of their hands,
flesh melted from its wicks; disintegrated cosmonauts, space
dogs
poisoned for the fall.

Through the natural processes of consumption
and disregard, humans make new mountains every year.
Take pleasure in the wilderness of unmown grass atop a land-
fill,
the cycle of short lives waving in the sun
rooted in the bodies that will last.

I could have been an archivist
whose sole purpose was to know where diaries were kept
and never read them.

See them catch the sunrise,
the PVC pipes studded on the mountain
for the exhausts of decay and bad reactions,
praising the mound like guardian stones, like dolmens,
like flag poles stripped of their nations

and showing only that here passed humans once
or something like them.
Who will dig through history's detritus
to find you?   Who
will pull themselves up into wakefulness
for you without knowing
first you were there?
This can be a good exercise.
This is too much to ask.

That blind sun.
I could have been that.

|Vigilance is the price of mercy.

I've moved out of my apartment and into the tangled nest
of panic and submission behind a horse's eyes.

Is this what you want? I could do something more
like a version of the Shield of Achilles,
in which the shield is brought up to date
in the form of a neck tattoo of a swan
eating another swan.

Every human body is a haunted house.
Do you ever smoke a lot not just because it will kill you
a little every time,
but also because cigarettes are a different kind of sundial
than even that? And force you to rehearse a trip outside
in which you will not come back?

I cherish walls, not fences you can reach your arm through.
For example, the great thing about a bonfire is that anything
that isn't light
is completely black.

You can trust that not hide itself in crevices and leak
into another room, not to linger in remission
like the smell in curtains you can't quite clean.

I owe texts all over town. Lists satisfy nothing anymore.

I'm BCCing you so you think
this message is going to everybody,
but it's not. There is a secret elect.
There is a silent broadcast into the brains
of the captains of humanity, the shepherds
who harvest the sheep, even when they are sleeping.
But here there is only me, emailing me,
worrying what you will think when you read it.

| Apoptosome.

I am dying for years in a leather chair of my own making
and the women still look
beautiful coming in and out of the butcher shop
on the ground floor, cheeks flush with ham, bodies built from
folios of poultry.
I am a thin woman and when she left me to pursue
other interests she mouthed,
"disputatious wraith,"
through the train car and through the window of the train,
mixing her last words and the silence on either side of them
all the way to me.

As if this thing being equal parts the opposites
said and *unsaid* was impregnable and everywhere at once,
covering past and future in dead skin.

It's not any sooner or the past, so this is just a version of my
life.
Pigs are intelligent creatures, hardly lesser, and would make
superb companions
when never leaving the apartment even once because you are in
love.

The way a rainstorm's first light
touch makes dirt bloom and give up
its fragrance.

I keep a red handkerchief for the sake of decorum, and yet I worship
this becoming

each day kneeling before my own body asking it what it will have
instead of me.

| Meat Clock

They would split your throat to cool themselves
in the midst of a great fire. They are your friends.

Bring them yellow tallboys in the plastic tub
you use to mop the bathroom, weave stories of your day

for them into a navy hammock, into sleep, all of you less
at work now, though never really off.

All the girls were track stars or masters of lacrosse.
Thoughts asked after the dimples of Venus

everywhere the way you'd wait for a song
you'd only heard a part of
to take over someone's radio and find you.

These days the same rent's due all month
and I study the suprasternal notch.
You can't do a thing like this with people

you don't fuck. Work
your fingers just above the ditch
where your collar bones would knock each other off

your body if they kept going
and you'll find the ribs of braided rope beneath the skin
inseparable from this precious neck.

It would be heaven to think. Wicked thing.
If we act like the things we want won't happen,
perhaps the universe will thwart us with success.

|Take comfort, Love.

When the moon hangs like a fang presume
there is another fang out there

past the Earth and this oceaned world
is just a drip of venom

on the serpent's lip.
In the meantime, no matter
where in the catalogue of sorrows,
orgasms, and miraculous contempt

a thing is found, you count it as important
if it would just happen to you once.
The clatter of bone as they bus
the coffee cups and saucers augurs
blank destruction. Make no sacrifice of the infant or the fist,
no one sees any of it, and there's no pity
from here to the scooped out moon,

which rises like a hammer or a newborn twin,
one more unconscious thing lifted for the kill.

Your mother's heart was a scar
she wore on her sleeve. Tell
the story. No. She told

me, as if telling me my flesh
could be as tender as the handle on a tool.

| There were days when the smell

of the river would lift
your eyes, even
with the sun's hand
pushing down your neck like one brother
pulling another's head to his.
Call from the bank
and hear the water teach itself
your language and your voice.

|3 Poems about Han Solo

Sex sideburned cowboy
jaguar — no seasons
argue in deep space

— — —

Gunslinger among
the electric samurai —
tight-pants astronaut

— — —

Man and bear thing tread
the naked face, the hungry moon —
this is what wookie means.

| You shall let your settled silt alone.

Like the time they were convinced that there were prom dates
in a car at the bottom of Panther Pond
and so they had to find a cannon
hoping the vast crack in the air above the waters
would draw them up.

My favorite parts of the Bible
are the ones my cousin made up
to induce me.
They are what God should have written.
They were what made God believable
and he used them to get me to reach into a leather bag
with chips of glass the ocean had smoothed over into waves
and give him the two coins with the face of JFK
I thought were hiding me from shadows.
He traded the only things that kept me safe
for ice cream.

I'm sure there were times when cathedrals
were the tallest thing around.
Towns and cow fields hung between them like phone lines.
I don't have to marry whoever I can anymore. I can drink
wine for whatever reason I want.
People will still think they
know why.

God said you could never own a thing
besides your mistakes,
and even some of those were passed down to you.
Where is his bed? Does he know what it's like
to forgive your friends for not showing up
when you're secretly very sad
like the wings
in stories we could let ourselves believe?

Do I have an empiric presence?
I step out onto the street and a homeless man
says "hey man can I have a bite of that?"
and I don't know what to say
because there is nothing in my hands.
It's night and I make eye contact
with the people at front desks
and know to stay on my side of the window.
It is such a relief to be certain in a godless world
sitting alone in my apartment
I can't let anybody down.

Any time is the time for the mind to give up her dead.
There's nothing I know my cousin said
since we were 13/but just
stop/they're firing
over panther pond again.

|Were You Not Meant to Live This Long

Flakes of Teflon mingle with the chicken's cuts
but I feel the elemental power of this chemical shale
no animal matter can stain
already. We should be lucky to absorb it, keep it
in our fat, our glands, our cavities.
We will be made stronger than all poison.
Relish, wicks, the hiss of the pan
like the first serpent promising all thoughts,
opening himself by rubbing scales off,
pink petals on the dirty ground.
Crack the earth and drink, my
little ones. If I were not meant
to teach you this, you would not be here.

| No Light No Heat

For the sake of argument, think of yourself
as a father sprinting across a bumper car rink
toward a child spinning backwards.
Do this and you will come to know the wisdom of carrying an
umbrella
to shield you from the sharp parts
of the other umbrellas on the street.

Six of Cups — reversed:
The one true God is a squirrel who drops
half a cranberry into your hair while you're thinking.
Say thank you. You smell fine.
Relationships elude you while they are happening
and you always have to stumble upon yourself mid-sentence
in the bathroom while you're talking to yourself
because you think someone has made you angry
and you are afraid to tell them,
but really they have just reminded you of how much
you are afraid
of yourself and you are afraid
to tell them.

How strange that generation after generation
of cells in your foot or elbow bow out to be replaced
but the language and the messengers you use

to teach them what you need
always stays the same.

Seven of Swords: Too many things held at once,
so no one will see you still have them, will split
you open at the palms.

How are you navigating the fear of others?
Loving is missing. It's hard to love you
when you're in the room.

Two of Wands: God throws a pinecone
at you as you think too much
about your ex.
A small one, though. Be grateful.
They're gone. The ice has split again before you,
the vision of the water underneath
will not leave for days.

| Holy are the disembodied.

He tries to stand up from the bed
to shave or find a window, to call out
or find a corner to be alone
with thoughts of what he's done or the marketplace or you.

Oh, but he is lost at sea.

The cloth of our white sails will fill your cups, set your tables,
block
the light of your bright windows, all your days.

But you had to know and we had to make sure someone told
you.
So it fell to us, as it always does, eyes fixed to the heart that's
behind you
watching you hear the words you surely knew were coming
since the first morning you awoke
and didn't seek his weight beside you.

| A Lake Considered as Discrete Drops

Clearly coffee is the secret ethos of your work
and with time and observation it is visible like a planet
that we come to know by moments when it dims a star.
It's not unlike watching your reflection in a window
until sun rises and there's just the world.

It's always been *we've made it, but:*
The morning houses animals you wouldn't breed.
The morning is never quite the coffee that could keep you
warm.

After rainstorms, a little wind
makes the trees cry.
In China closing shops play Kenny G
as a way of asking you to leave.
A jetliner returns to the earth
as a perfect snow of lotus petals.

People are cruel, especially when they don't know
what they want or why
they are afraid.

It's mercy that the same sun rolls toward us every day
from everywhere else that people are, from all the human days
that have ever been
but carries nothing of them with it.

| Point is:

ComeonSWOON with me, Margo!
He waits through a most
serious martyring: "Here are some obsidian tips, son,
now don
't let us catch ya doin' it again"
and still he lays there for Irene
of Rome until she slouches
over to the ditch
all dark and *Flemish*
to pull on a relic or two
commit dust to something
and under the sheet she brought he shakes out, "Jigger my
quills a bit, dear,
they're brand new but I fear
the shafts have gone all crooked."

This morning I slid out
from between my sheets
a still-born calf, mouth full of last night
gone sour and I'm not nearly as startled
by people splitting up into conversation.

After they put the arrows in Saint Sebastian,
we waited to catch his breath again.

He went back and said something like, "You didn't do it right. Fix it or I might be gone for good."

| Hypertrophic Cardiac Myopathy

Bodies beyond the touch of chaos, young runners
win their races and then fall into the grass beyond the track
like lovers jumping back under the covers after breakfast
never to be seen again,

killed out of nowhere by part their own heart
growing too strong to use, an embarrassment
of lightning.

The wikipedia article says "sudden death" a lot.

Dad's pop called him Jasper because his real name was John.
My siblings named me Cooper. My father calls me Jasper
so the name lives on.

How much of the message of your DNA
will your kid remember as his face,
as how she walls her hands around a paper cup
of vending machine coffee in a hospital cafeteria slash gift
shop?

Philippides was a "day runner"
who died when he was exactly 40,
which is the only record he'd ever existed at all.
That, and Athens somewhat.

I'm picturing a daughter I may never have
and the kind of cup I've only seen in Judgement Day,
the one ringed off with playing cards
the officer on duty gets and knows he's won
right before the T-1000 Terminator shaped just like a cop
pierces his brain and copies him completely.

In 1982 three pilots of the British airforce, all named John,
tried to run the same way Philippides did from Marathon
in one day and change. The same race 3000 years on,
and they all did it, but not quite the same.
None of them died in the end.

They had no messages to save.
But I am not the one who's dying either.
At a research facility under Tufts
they have planted a defibrillator smaller than a house key
into my father's chest
as an electric fence to nudge him back
every time his life begins to wander off.

Somehow the computer knows
when it is needed. Strange to think
I would ask for this
if I knew who I could ever ask
for my one job.

| Hydrogen hums red when torn.

Love puts holes in things.
Walls for example, 5-year plans, checking accounts,
Sundays. The capacity for suffering

is a prerequisite for light,
even for the things that can not burn.
Batteries release the scream
of rust, of one thing retching electrons from another
in a soup that nourishes
the speed of their decay.

Despite everything, my parents raised me.
They even loved me. These things
should always be surprising.

The end of the world is coming
every single day. You have choices to make
even though it looks like they won't matter.

The world has always been abandoned,
draughty, cursed, the crops
aborted, oozing black out of the ground,
the children enslaved and weighed down
with parasites. The only clean things
humans make are bones.

I've written so many poems
pretending to be a person I'm not,
because I am those people.

You can wrap your mind around a loss and make
a cozy little room to spend your life in.
Only nothing is perfect, especially an absence unobserved

The universe is baffling, mass baffling,
light baffling, baffling stones, baffling ice.
Baffling man and baffling woman and baffling wave
and baffling island risen over centuries then gone.
Zeros have no corners. Gone makes
perfect sense.

There wasn't supposed to be anyone
and even there being someone, it was not
supposed to be me.

Dad got the surgery that apparently didn't work.
There's no reason I should be here,
but that doesn't mean I shouldn't be here.

You can choose at any time to be a candle,
and the time in need of candles came
before our parents ever opened up their lungs
and gave space within them to this world.

Acknowledgements

Many thanks to the following publications in which versions of these poems have appeared and to their editors: *Adirondack Review*; *Arc*; *Cosmonauts Avenue*; *Drunk In A Midnight Choir*; *FIVE:2:ONE*; *FLAPPERHOUSE*; *Luna Luna*; *The Mackinac*; *Moonsick Magazine*; *The Moth*; *The Opiate; Queen Mob's Tea House*; *Reality Beach*; *Red Branch Journal*; *Rogue Agent*; *Rust + Moth*; *#the-sideshow*; *Vanilla Sex Magazine*; and *Yes, Poetry*.

Also thank you to my editor, Joanna Valente, for marvelous suggestions and for believing in this book; to Michael J. Seidlinger at CCM; to Grace Linderholm for their patience and insight with these poems; to Katie Longofono, Devin Kelly, Lisa Marie Basile, David Shreve; Michelle Taylor, Claire Wallace, and Garrett Fiddler; to Jess Martinez and Stacey Kahn for making New York make sense as a place for me to be a writer and human person; to Richard Deming; to Ilan Ben-Meir; to Bijan Stephen; to Peter Gizzi; to the Roman god Mercury (you know what you did); to Mom and Pop for supporting me; to God and Satan (you know what you did); to all the ghosts and flowers; and to the woman in the car who told me about Glenn Danzig and about giving birth.

OFFICIAL

CCM ◕

GET OUT OF JAIL
* VOUCHER *

- -

Tear this out.
Skip that social event.
It's okay.
You don't have to go if you don't want to. Pick up
the book you just bought. Open to the first page.
You'll thank us by the third paragraph.

If friends ask why you were a no-show, show them
this voucher.
You'll be fine.

- -

We're coping.

◕

Made in the USA
Middletown, DE
02 January 2019